CLASS IN AMERICA

CLASS
MOBILITY

BY DUCHESS HARRIS, JD, PHD
WITH ELISABETH HERSCHBACH

Essential Library

An Imprint of Abdo Publishing | abdopublishing.com

ABDOPUBLISHING.COM

Published by Abdo Publishing, a division of ABDO, PO Box 398166, Minneapolis, Minnesota 55439.
Copyright © 2019 by Abdo Consulting Group, Inc. International copyrights reserved in all countries.
No part of this book may be reproduced in any form without written permission from the publisher.
Essential Library™ is a trademark and logo of Abdo Publishing.

Printed in the United States of America, North Mankato, Minnesota
032018
092018

**THIS BOOK CONTAINS
RECYCLED MATERIALS**

Cover Photo: Derek Brumby/Shutterstock Images
Interior Photos: Erik McGregor/Sipa USA/Newscom, 5, 91; Paul Sancya/AP Images, 7; Kydpl Kyodo/
AP Images, 12; Sipa USA-FG/Newscom, 15; iStockphoto, 18, 29, 36–37, 72–73, 97; D. M. Baker/
iStockphoto, 20–21; Red Line Editorial, 27, 31; Erik McGregor/Sipa USA/AP Images, 32; Stefan
Rousseau/PA Wire URN:34213457/AP Images, 35; Matt Rourke/AP Images, 41; Charles Dharapak/AP
Images, 43; Brandy Taylor/iStockphoto, 46; Biz Jones Image Source/Newscom, 48–49; Seth Wenig/
AP Images, 53; Juan Monino/iStockphoto, 54; Monkey Business Images/iStockphoto, 58; Sergi
Reboredo/Alamy, 61; Elise Amendola/AP Images, 67; Jean Pieri/Pioneer Press/AP Images, 70; Mary
Altaffer/AP Images, 76; Manuel Balce Ceneta/AP Images, 79; Kamil Krzaczynski/AP Images, 82–83;
Wave Break Media/Shutterstock Images, 84; John Minchillo/AP Images, 87; REX/Shutterstock, 94–95

Editor: Alyssa Krekelberg
Series Designer: Becky Daum

LIBRARY OF CONGRESS CONTROL NUMBER: 2017961141

PUBLISHER'S CATALOGING-IN-PUBLICATION DATA

Names: Harris, Duchess, author. | Herschbach, Elisabeth, author.
Title: Class mobility / by Duchess Harris and Elisabeth Herschbach.
Description: Minneapolis, Minnesota : Abdo Publishing, 2019. | Series: Class in America | Includes
      online resources and index.
Identifiers: ISBN 9781532114076 (lib.bdg.) | ISBN 9781532153907 (ebook)
Subjects: LCSH: Occupational mobility--Juvenile literature. | United States--Social policy--Juvenile
      literature. | Race relations--Juvenile literature. | Social classes--Juvenile literature. | Social
      classes--United States--History--Juvenile literature.
Classification: DDC 301.451--dc23

CONTENTS

ONE

A DIVIDED
NATION

O n April 15, 2015, approximately 60,000 workers in more than 200 cities around the country walked off their jobs and took to the streets.[1] They began the largest protest by low-wage workers in US history. The protesters included fast-food workers, Walmart employees, childcare assistants, home health-care aides, workers at airports, gas stations, and convenience stores, and even some professors.

Their specific goals were to rally for a higher minimum wage, better working conditions, and the right to form unions. Their general goal was to draw attention to economic inequalities in the United States—inequalities that, according to many researchers, are making it increasingly difficult for both

In 2017, groups of workers continued protesting for an increase in the minimum wage.

low-wage workers and middle-class Americans to move up the economic ladder.

"We are forcing a real conversation about how to solve the grossest inequality in our generation," said Mary Kay Henry, the international president of the Service Employees International Union, which backed the protests. "People are sick of wealth at the top and no accountability for corporations."[2]

THE RICH AND THE SUPERRICH

The United States' wealth gap is often described by comparing the economic assets of the top one percent of people with those of the bottom 99 percent. However, economist Paul Krugman argues this actually understates the extent of economic disparity in the United States. The vast amount of wealth in the United States is actually concentrated in the hands of an even smaller elite—the top 0.1 percent of the one percent, or the richest one-thousandth of Americans. These superrich Americans now control a whopping 22 percent of the United States' wealth, up from approximately 7 percent in 1979.[5]

THE HAVES AND THE HAVE-NOTS

Roughly 15 million children in the United States grow up in households at or below the federal poverty line. That's approximately one in five US children.[3] More than 52 million Americans live in neighborhoods that are considered economically distressed.[4] These are neighborhoods with low high school graduation rates, high levels of poverty and unemployment, low median incomes, and shrinking job prospects.

At the same time, the United States boasts the world's largest number of billionaires. Together, these 540 billionaires have a net worth of approximately $2.4 trillion, representing 12 percent of the US gross domestic product (GDP). The United

Many businesses in Detroit, Michigan, closed after the economy faced struggles in 2008. The city has one of the highest poverty rates in the United States.

States' richest billionaire, Microsoft cofounder Bill Gates, has a net worth of $89 billion.[6] His net worth is more than double the GDP of Lithuania, a country in Europe. With a net worth of more than $86 billion, Amazon founder Jeff Bezos, the United States' second-wealthiest billionaire, could afford to buy every single one of the 136,000 houses in his home city of Seattle, Washington.[7]

A WIDENING GAP

According to economist Thomas Piketty, income inequality in the United States "is probably higher than in any other society at any

WEALTH AND INCOME: WHAT'S THE DIFFERENCE?

People often use the terms interchangeably, but *wealth* and *income* mean different things. Wealth refers to a person's net worth, or the total value of his or her assets, minus any debts. Income is the amount of money that a person receives on a regular basis. Wages and salaries from a job are the most common sources of income. Other sources of income include stocks, retirement pensions, social security benefits, sales revenues, and rents from property. People can have a high income without being wealthy. For example, this might happen if they have a lot of debts and their cost of living is high. And people can be wealthy without having a high income. For example, they may have inherited so much wealth that they don't need a paycheck. There is more wealth inequality than income inequality in the United States because wealth accumulates over time and is passed on from generation to generation. As a result, the wealth gap increases over time. Economist Gregory Clark argues that the lingering effects of wealth can last for generations.

time in the past, anywhere in the world."[8] But the income gap in the United States is not only big—it's growing.

Since 1980, the wealthiest one percent of Americans have doubled their share of the national income. By contrast, Americans in the bottom 50 percent have seen almost no growth in their incomes. In the 1970s, the nation's top-earning executives made 23 times the wages of the average worker. By 2000, they were making 120 times more.[9] Today, some chief executive officers (CEOs) in the United States make 271 times more than the average employee—an eye-popping $15.6 million a year.[10]

Combined, the 400 people on *Forbes* magazine's list of richest Americans own more wealth than all of the approximately 194 million people in the bottom 61 percent of the country put together.[11] The six heirs to the Walmart empire have as much wealth as the poorest 42 percent of Americans put together—a staggering $90 billion.[12] And the wealthiest one percent of Americans pocket nearly

POVERTY WAGES

Out of the 35 member countries of the Organisation for Economic Co-operation and Development (OECD), the United States ranks third for income. Only workers in Luxembourg and Norway enjoy higher average incomes. But the United States is only in 18th place for people in the bottom 10 percent of the income distribution. For every $100 that the average citizen of an OECD country makes, the average American makes $123. But the poorest 10 percent of Americans make only $73 for every $100 earned by their counterparts in other OECD countries.[13]

25 percent of the nation's income and control 40 percent of the wealth.[14]

THE PRICE OF POVERTY

These imbalances are connected with many other inequalities, including unequal access to education, employment opportunities, and health care. Residents of low-income communities are exposed to more environmental pollutants and toxins. They suffer from higher rates of obesity and diabetes. Asthma is 60 percent more common among poor children than among those who are not poor.[15] Learning disabilities are almost twice as common.

Low-income Americans are not only unhealthier than wealthy Americans. They also live shorter lives. On average, in the United States the poorest one percent of men live almost 15 fewer years than the richest one percent of men.[16] Their life expectancy is comparable with the average life expectancy in some developing countries.

THE GREAT GATSBY CURVE

Economists refer to the correlation between increasing economic inequality and decreasing economic mobility as the Great Gatsby Curve. This name was inspired by F. Scott Fitzgerald's 1925 novel, *The Great Gatsby*, which explored class divisions and social mobility in the United States. Alan Krueger, a Princeton University economist who served as chair of the Council of Economic Advisors in the Barack Obama administration, coined the term in 2012. He observed the correlation between inequality and social mobility in data collected by Miles Corak, a professor of economics at Ottawa University.

GETTING TO THE TOP

Economists and policy analysts agree that economic inequality is on the rise in the United States. However, there is disagreement about what this trend means for the country. Some analysts argue that economic equality—how equally or unequally income is distributed—is not what matters. Instead, they argue, what Americans care about is economic mobility—the ability to move from one income group to another. Bruce R. Bartlett, an economist who served in the Ronald Reagan and George H. W. Bush administrations, said, "As long as people think they have a chance of getting to the top, they just don't care how rich the rich are."[17]

DEFINING POVERTY

Every year, the US Department of Health and Human Services sets a federal poverty threshold. Individuals or families are considered to be in poverty if their annual income falls below that threshold. In 2017, the threshold was $12,060 for an individual, $16,240 for a family of two, and $24,600 for a family of four.[18] By those cutoffs, almost 13 percent of Americans are in poverty.[19] Approximately 45 percent of them are living in what is considered extreme poverty. This is defined as having a total cash income below 50 percent of the poverty threshold. Close to 20 million people live in extreme poverty, according to 2015 US census estimates. That comes to approximately 6 percent of the total US population.[20] However, many researchers argue that the number of poor Americans is actually much higher than these estimates suggest. Critics say the measures used to define poverty are flawed because they are based on outdated assumptions about the cost of living. They also fail to account for variations in the cost of living across the nation. As a result, federal poverty statistics significantly underestimate the true number of poor Americans.

But international research suggests that economic equality and economic mobility are linked. Countries with more economic equality enjoy higher rates of mobility between generations. Parents' incomes and social statuses play less of a role in determining where their children will end up on the economic ladder as adults. Conversely, countries with greater inequality have less mobility. Children's outcomes are shaped to a greater degree by advantages and disadvantages inherited from their parents. As a report by the Organisation for Economic

The OECD brings government officials from around the world together to talk about economic and environmental problems. Yuriko Koike, the governor of Tokyo, Japan, participated in a 2017 lecture.

Co-operation and Development (OECD) put it, "Rising income inequality . . . can stifle upward social mobility, making it harder for talented and hard-working people to get the rewards they deserve."[21]

Many researchers see this pattern at work in the United States. Economic mobility appears to have stalled or even declined over the last generation. The result, as former president Barack Obama put it in a 2013 speech, is "a dangerous and growing inequality and lack of upward mobility that has jeopardized middle-class America's basic bargain—that if you work hard, you have a chance to get ahead."[22]

DISCUSSION STARTERS

- Bruce R. Bartlett argues that Americans don't care about the gap between the rich and the poor as long as they have a chance to get to the top. Do you agree or disagree? Why?

- Why do you think that asthma is 60 percent more common among poor children than it is among wealthy children? What environmental factors might explain this finding?

- Why do you think the life expectancy between wealthy people and poor people is different?

TWO

CLASS CONSTRAINTS
AND CLASS
MOBILITY

T he idea that everyone should have an equal chance to succeed is a key part of people's sense of fairness. A society in which people's opportunities are limited by chance factors, such as the color of their skin, seems unfair to many people. So does a society in which people's economic prospects are determined by their birth. In 2007, former Federal Reserve chair Ben Bernanke noted that equality of opportunity is an important concept in the United States.

MOVING ON UP

One way that researchers measure economic opportunity is to track intergenerational mobility, or movement between economic classes from one generation to the next. Greater opportunity creates a more level playing field. It decreases the

Ben Bernanke has noted that the lack of class mobility is an issue in the United States.

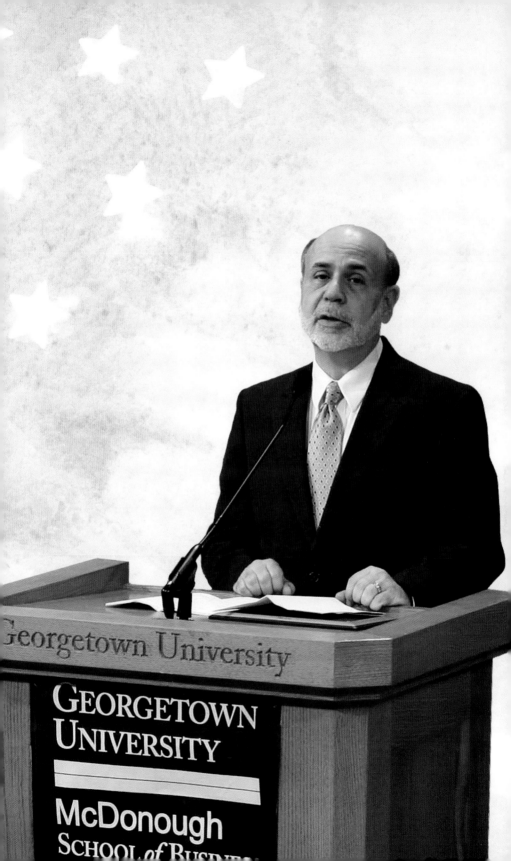

extent to which people's starting positions in life predict or restrict where they can end up as adults.

In a society with a lot of equality of opportunity, people can expect a lot of movement between economic classes. Children from poor families will be just as likely as children from rich families to end up at the top of the economic ladder when they are adults, and vice versa. In a society with less equality of opportunity, there will be less movement up and down the economic ladder. Throughout their lives, people are likely to remain in the same economic class as their parents. Economists call this stickiness.

ADAMS AND THE AMERICAN DREAM

Historian James Truslow Adams is credited with originating the term *American dream*. In his 1931 book, *The Epic of America*, he noted the American dream has drawn millions of people across the world to the United States. He also mentioned that the dream includes the belief that people have the opportunity to succeed.

A LAND OF OPPORTUNITY?

Americans have traditionally viewed the United States as a fluid, open society with few rigid class barriers. This view forms the core of the American dream. The American dream is a vision of the United States as a uniquely mobile society—a land of opportunity where anyone can get ahead if he or she works hard.

Surveys show that faith in the American dream remains strong. In a 2009 poll conducted by the Pew Charitable Trusts, the majority of people said that personal attributes such as intelligence, perseverance, and skills matter more for getting ahead than coming from a wealthy family. A 2005 *New York Times* poll found that 75 percent of Americans think that the chances of moving up to a higher class are either the same as or greater than they were 30 years ago. And more than 45 percent think that it is easier to move to a higher social class in the United States than in Europe.[1]

Republican congressman Paul Ryan of Wisconsin echoed this optimism in a 2011 speech. "Class is not a fixed designation in this country," he said. "We are an upwardly mobile society with a lot of movement between income groups." He went on to contrast the United States with the "top-heavy welfare states" of Europe, where "masses of the long-term unemployed are locked into the new lower class."[2]

Statistics suggest a different reality. Despite the traditional

REALITY GAP

Americans are not only optimistic about their chances for mobility; they are also more optimistic than people in countries with greater actual rates of upward mobility such as Canada. For example, in a 2009 Pew survey, less than one-half of Americans said that financial success is tied to parents' incomes, compared with more than one-half of Canadians. Similarly, in an international survey across 27 nations, 69 percent of Americans agreed that "people are rewarded for intelligence and skill," compared with an international median of less than 40 percent for the other nations.[3]

Regardless of how hard children work in the United States, they will likely have the same class status as their parents.

view of the United States as a land of boundless opportunity, Americans today are less upwardly mobile than they were in the 1960s and 1970s. They also enjoy less economic mobility than the citizens of many other developed nations. In fact, the socioeconomic class children are born into appears to play a bigger role in their status as adults in the United States than it does in Europe. As Nobel Prize–winning economist Joseph Stiglitz notes, children's outcomes in the United States depend more on their parents' economic class than they do in almost any other advanced country.

LIKE FATHER, LIKE SON

Economists estimate the extent to which family background constrains individuals' economic opportunities. They do this by dividing a population into quintiles, or five equal parts, by average household income. Then, they calculate a person's economic class compared with the rest of the population. They compare a person's economic class with the relative economic class attained by his or her parents at a similar stage of life. This gives people an estimate of relative mobility, or the extent to which people move up and down the economic ladder relative to their parents' generation.

Economists measure relative mobility by calculating what they call intergenerational elasticity, sometimes also referred to as income heritability. The resulting score, on a scale of zero to one, gives people an estimate of the relative stickiness of a society, or the extent to which children are likely to inherit the relative economic status of their parents.

A lower number means less stickiness and more mobility. For example, an elasticity score of zero would mean that children's economic prospects are not constrained at all by their family backgrounds. The closer a country's score gets to one, the higher the correlation between family background and economic outcomes. In other words, higher scores mean that it is harder to move outside of the economic class one is born into.

On average, an elasticity score of 0.4 means that parents pass on 40 percent of their relative economic advantage or disadvantage to their children. For example, parents who earn $20,000 more than the mean income will, on average, have children who earn $8,000 more than the mean when they grow up. Parents who earn $20,000 less will have children

who earn $8,000 less when they grow up. According to some estimates, US income elasticity ranges from 0.5 to as high as 0.6.[4] These scores represent a significant correlation between parents' incomes and their children's incomes as adults.

To put the United States' estimates into context, Canada's elasticity score is 0.19, meaning that parents pass on only 19 percent of their income level to their children. Denmark, the nation with the highest level of income mobility, has an intergenerational income elasticity of 0.15. A long list of other countries also outperform the United States in comparative studies of mobility, including Australia, Norway, Finland, Sweden, Germany, the Netherlands, Spain, France, Switzerland, Japan, New Zealand, Singapore, and Pakistan.[5]

As Miles Corak, an economist at the University of Ottawa in Canada, puts it, "Children are much more likely as adults to end up in the same place on the income and status ladder as their parents in the United States than

NO PLACE LIKE HOME

Owning a home has traditionally been considered an important symbol of achieving the American dream. However, the rate of homeownership in the United States has fallen to its lowest level since 1965, according to the Pew Research Center, which is a nonpartisan research organization that conducts public opinion polling. Instead, many people rent. Most renters say that they currently rent as a result of circumstances rather than because of personal preference. A majority of these renters cite financial reasons.

in most other countries."[6] This is especially true at the extremes of the economic ladder.

EXTREME STICKINESS

The middle-class experience remains fairly fluid in the United States, although there is more downward mobility than upward mobility. Approximately 36 percent of Americans raised in the middle quintile move up the economic ladder as adults. Forty-one percent move down. Twenty-three percent stay at the same income level as their parents.[7]

However, researchers have found that there is a particularly high degree of stickiness at the very top and bottom rungs of the economic ladder in the United States. Almost one-half of Americans from the lowest income quintile stay there as adults. By comparison, the percentages range from 25 to 30 percent for Denmark, Finland, Sweden, Norway, and the United Kingdom.[8] Less than 5 percent of the poorest Americans make it all the way to the top as adults. In Denmark, this number is 14 percent.[9]

At the other extreme of the economic ladder, less than one-half of American children raised in the top fifth of incomes remain at the same level as adults. The majority of these children remain in the top two-fifths. Only a small percentage fall all the way to the bottom. In other words, the poorest Americans tend to stay poor, and the richest tend to stay rich.

RELATIVE AND ABSOLUTE MOBILITY

Relative mobility looks at a person's economic position relative to others and compares it with where his or her parents stood on the economic ladder relative to his or her own generation. However, some critics argue that this is not a meaningful way to gauge how well people are doing in an economy. They argue instead that it's more important to consider whether people have more or less money than their parents had when they were the same age. This is known as absolute mobility.

Reihan Salam, executive editor of the conservative political magazine *National Review*, argues that "relative mobility is overrated as a social policy goal."[10] Instead, he notes that people should focus on increasing overall prosperity.

Similarly, Neil Gilbert, a professor at the University of California, Berkeley, argues that "rather than comparing how one's income ranks relative to others all across the country, it would be wiser to focus on an absolute measure of social mobility, one that describes an individual's changing level of prosperity over time." Economic growth raises living standards across the board. This means that people in the lowest income brackets today may be making more money than their parents did at the same age. In Gilbert's view, these absolute gains in income matter more to us than "how the neighbors are doing" because they make a greater difference to our level of material comfort.[11]

A FADING DREAM

However, even when people look at absolute mobility instead of relative mobility, there are reasons to worry. Overall rates of absolute upward income mobility have dropped steeply since 1940. The vast majority of Americans born in 1940 earned more than their parents. For Americans born in 1980, only approximately one-half were earning more than their parents. And for the youngest generation in the labor force today, the promise of upward mobility appears to be slipping away altogether. Today, people born after 1980 have an average income that is significantly lower than that of their parents.

DISCUSSION STARTERS

- Why do you think some people believe the United States has more upward class mobility than European countries?

- In your view, how important for success are hard work, education, natural ability, the right connections, wealth, and income?

- Andrew Carnegie, a steel industrialist in the 1800s, was born in a one-room cottage to a poor Scottish weaver. He started working at the age of 13, changing spools of thread in a cotton factory for $1.20 per week. By the end of his life, he had become one of the richest Americans of all time. Do you think that rags-to-riches stories such as this can tell us anything about achieving the American dream?

LOST EINSTEINS

Most Americans agree that talent and hard work should matter more to success than how much money a family has. That's a key part of the American dream. But does reality live up to the dream?

Researchers at the Equality of Opportunity Project—a collaboration of economists studying mobility—came up with an interesting approach to the question. They linked tax records, patent applications, and scores on elementary school math tests to see how family income affects children's chances of becoming inventors. The data showed that children who were good in math were much more likely to grow up to be inventors. But the results also showed that math achievement wasn't enough. Family income mattered a great deal, too. In fact, low-income students who were among the highest achievers in math were no more likely to become inventors than below-average math students from high-income families. This results in many "lost Einsteins," as the researchers put it. These are children who could have produced great innovations if they had been allowed to live up to their potential. This isn't just unfair. It is also bad for society. This is because, as the researchers note, "innovation is widely viewed as the engine of economic growth."[12]

INVENTIONS AS LINKED TO PARENT INCOME[13]

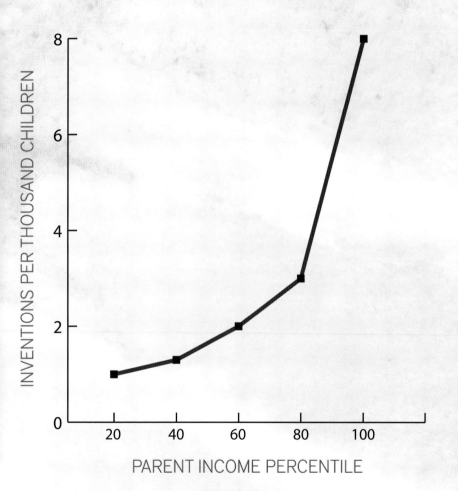

THREE

INEQUALITY AND
UPWARD
MOBILITY

C lass mobility was not always low in the United States. Traveling through the United States in the 1830s, the historian and sociologist Alexis de Tocqueville observed a land of exceptional mobility, free from fixed class divisions. He noted European families were not economically mobile. However, he saw that in the United States people were able to change their economic status.

At the time Tocqueville was writing, the majority of sons of unskilled laborers in the United States were able to move up to better jobs than their fathers had, according to economist Joseph Ferrie. In Britain, by contrast, only one-half were able to move up. Even well into the 1900s, the United States continued to live up to its reputation as a land of opportunity, where citizens enjoyed

Some people are unable to climb the economic ladder.

higher rates of mobility compared with those of other nations. So, what happened?

SHRINKING SLICES OF THE ECONOMIC PIE

Economists point to two general trends correlated with the decline in mobility. First, wages have stagnated and economic growth has slowed since the mid-1970s. Second, most of the growth that has occurred has been distributed very unevenly. The biggest share by far has gone to those at the top. Imagine the United States had 100 citizens and all the wealth amounted to 100 pieces of pie. Instead of having an even distribution between citizens, the richest one person is taking more and more slices of the economic pie, leaving less for everyone else.

GROWING PAINS

Gross domestic product (GDP) is the total value of goods and services produced in a country over a period of time. It serves as an indicator of how much a country's economy is growing. Until approximately 1974, the US GDP grew at a healthy average of 3.8 percent per year. In 2016, US economic growth slowed down to a sluggish 1.6 percent per year.[1]

Slower economic growth affects mobility because it limits the overall number of opportunities that are available. It can also cause wages to stagnate. But of the two trends, growing inequality is much more significant. This is because, when inequality grows, the people at the bottom will still end up with a shrinking slice even if the overall size of the pie increases.

ECONOMIC PIE²

The economic pie analogy shows how uneven the distribution of wealth is in the United States. This analogy divides wealth into 100 pieces of pie. This model shows that the richest Americans hold most of the wealth and illuminates the wealth gap in the United States.

People with an average net worth of $3 million hold 90 slices of pie.

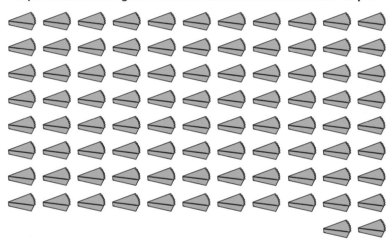

People with an average net worth of $273,600 hold 8 slices of pie.

People with an average net worth of $81,700 hold 2 slices of pie.

People with an average net worth of -$8,900 hold 0 slices of pie.

This shows why relative mobility is an important indicator of economic well-being. Because inequality has risen dramatically in the United States over the past few generations, relative economic standing comes with high stakes. A person's starting rung on the economic ladder carries enormous weight.

OUTCOMES AND OPPORTUNITIES

Economic equality and equality of opportunity are distinct concepts. Economic equality has to do with outcomes—the distribution of wealth and income among people. Equality of opportunity has to do with prospects for achieving certain

The growing income gap between rich and poor Americans has angered many people.

outcomes—whether there is a level playing field so that people from different backgrounds, given equal skill and effort, have an equal chance to succeed.

Some degree of economic inequality is inevitable. People have different skills, interests, and abilities, and these will lead to different outcomes. In a meritocratic society that rewards skill and effort, some will rise higher than others. These inequalities of outcome can provide an incentive to work hard and succeed.

The problem occurs when economic inequality spirals out of control. Although outcomes and opportunities are not the same thing, they are related. The distribution of income in one generation may affect the opportunities of the next generation. And when the gaps between the haves and the have-nots get too big, prospects for upward mobility start to decline. This erodes the sense of

WHY HAS ECONOMIC INEQUALITY INCREASED?

Why has economic inequality increased so much in the United States in the past few decades? Economists have considered a range of factors. One factor is the United States' especially high rate of poverty. Another is that technological changes, trade, outsourcing of jobs overseas, and globalization have created a lower demand—and hence fewer jobs and lower wages—for low-skill workers. At the same time, unions have become less powerful, giving workers less of a voice. Government policies, such as tax structures that disproportionately benefit the wealthy, also play an important role.

MEASURING INEQUALITY

One way that economists measure inequality is with the Gini coefficient, named after Italian sociologist and statistician Corrado Gini. The Gini coefficient measures the dispersion of income or wealth across groups on a scale of zero to one. Zero represents perfect equality, and one represents perfect inequality. According to the 2016 Allianz Global Wealth Report, the United States has a wealth inequality score of .81.[3] This was the highest level of wealth inequality of the 53 countries studied. For income inequality, the United States has a Gini coefficient of .39, the fourth-highest score after Turkey, Chile, and Mexico.[4]

a fair society with equality of opportunity—a society in which merit and effort are rewarded and wealth is not just inherited. Best-selling author J. D. Vance said that if people believe it's hard to succeed, they will wonder whether it's even worth trying to get ahead. The costs of this mentality are not just social. They are also economic.

SPREADING THE WEALTH

A popular argument is that inequality actually stimulates the economy and leads to greater overall prosperity. For example, in his book *Popular Economics: What the Rolling Stones, Downton Abbey, and LeBron James Can Teach You about Economics*, John Tamny argues that the ideal way to spread wealth is to leave the money with wealthy people. This general approach is known as trickle-down economics. It advocates policies that benefit the wealthy, such as reducing their taxes, with the idea that this will stimulate the economy and benefit everyone else in the long run.

Clothing is one example of a consumer good that, when purchased by consumers, helps pump money into the economy.

However, the emerging consensus among economists is that the opposite is true. Studies show the way that income and wealth are distributed in a society—how well or poorly off people are in relation to each other—actually affects economic growth. When inequality gets too high, economic growth slows. Conversely, when the economic rewards are spread more evenly, sustained economic growth is more likely.

Research from the International Monetary Fund (IMF), an organization of more than 100 member countries that promotes economic growth and international trade, backs this up. For example, in a 2015 IMF study, the main takeaway was that "increasing the income share of the poor and the middle class actually increases growth while a rising income share of the top 20 percent results in lower growth—that is, when the rich get richer, benefits do not trickle down."[5] Similarly, a 2014 OECD report concluded that the "single biggest impact on growth is the widening gap between the lower middle class and poor households compared to the rest of society."[6]

A CONSUMPTION PROBLEM

Why does increased economic inequality end up obstructing economic growth in the long run? One reason has to do with what economists call the marginal propensity to consume, or rates of consumption. People associate the superrich with extravagant spending. But despite the luxury yachts, designer clothes, private jets, and mansions, the very wealthy actually

MONEY TALKS

The richest one percent of Americans may be reaping big rewards from the United States' skewed income and wealth distribution. However, some of the nation's wealthiest billionaires are worried about the growing divide. For example, billionaire Bill Gates noted that inequality is an issue. He said that high levels of it hurts the economy and the idea that people are equal. Warren Buffett, the world's fourth-richest man, noted in a *PBS NewsHour* interview that the United States is failing its poorest citizens. "The American dream has been very real for millions and millions of people over the years," he said, "but there has been an American nightmare that has accompanied that, and that's where people who equally tried to get educated and worked hard and had good habits . . . found themselves living a life that's been on the edge throughout their entire lives and the same for their children."[7]

spend a smaller portion of their overall income than people with lower incomes do.

When extra income is put in the hands of low- and middle-income people, they tend to spend a greater portion of it on consumer goods. Therefore, more of that income ends up back in the economy. This stimulates growth and job creation. In contrast, when extra income is put in the hands of the wealthy, the bulk of it is likely to end up as private assets and savings. Instead of being pumped back into the economy, it stays in the hands of the rich.

DISCUSSION STARTERS

- Do you think it's fair that some people have more slices of the economic pie than others? Explain your answer.

- Based on the information in this chapter, what are some reasons for thinking that trickle-down economics doesn't work?

- The term *snowball effect* is used to describe a process that builds upon itself, increasing or intensifying as it goes along in a self-perpetuating cycle. According to economists Emmanuel Saez and Gabriel Zucman, income inequality creates a snowball effect on the distribution of wealth. In what way do you think that might be true? How might a country stop the cycle?

FOUR

THE GEOGRAPHY
OF MOBILITY

O verall, upward mobility in the United States has declined since the 1970s. Yet when researchers compare different regions of the country, it turns out that intergenerational mobility varies significantly across geographical areas. In some areas of the country, upward mobility is actually quite high.

In other words, just as there are growing income and wealth gaps in the United States, there is also a mobility gap. Depending on which area of the country they are born into, some Americans enjoy a greater likelihood than others of moving up from the socioeconomic class in which they were born. Stanford University economist Raj Chetty and colleagues noted that there are areas within the United States that give people opportunities,

Philadelphia, Pennsylvania, had a poverty rate of 25.8 percent in 2015.

but there are also areas where children are forced into a cycle of poverty.

MAPPING MOBILITY

Across the United States, family background strongly affects economic outcomes. In general, incomes of parents and children are highly correlated. This suggests that the socioeconomic class one is born into significantly affects where one ends up on the economic ladder as an adult. However, in different geographical areas, the magnitude of that effect is strikingly different.

For example, children born into the lowest income bracket in Charlotte, North Carolina, have less than a 5 percent chance of making it into the highest income bracket when they are adults. In contrast, in Salt Lake City, Utah, children from the bottom income bracket have a more than 10 percent chance of moving up to the top bracket as adults. In San Jose, California, the chance is even higher.[1]

MOVING FOR MOBILITY

Economists Raj Chetty and Nathaniel Hendren analyzed data on millions of children who moved to different neighborhoods while growing up. They documented the effects of neighborhoods on children's outcomes in life. Compared with their peers in high-poverty neighborhoods, low-income children who move to higher-mobility neighborhoods perform better academically, are more likely to attend college, and are less likely to become teen parents. As adults, they earn more. Chetty and Hendren estimate that every year of exposure to a better environment improves a child's prospects for success.

Organizations such as DC Promise Neighborhood Initiative are trying to improve Kenilworth-Parkside in Washington, DC, and other communities by eliminating intergenerational poverty.

In some areas of the United States, levels of relative mobility actually match or even exceed those of countries with the highest overall mobility rates, such as Canada and Denmark. In some parts of Iowa, the probability of climbing from the bottom fifth to the top fifth of income distribution is as high as 15 or 16 percent. However, other areas have mobility levels below those of any other developed nation for which data are available. For example, in Atlanta, Georgia, the probability of moving from the lowest to the highest income quintile plunges to 4.5 percent.[2]

A FRAGMENTED LANDSCAPE

Researchers have found that, in general, the American Southeast has the lowest relative mobility rates in the country. The West and rural Midwest enjoy the country's highest rates. However, even within broad geographical regions there are sharp differences at the local level. In Chicago, Illinois, children raised in low-income families earn less at age 30 than their counterparts from rural areas of the state. In San Francisco, California, children from the lowest income bracket have approximately twice the chance of moving up to the top bracket when they are adults that their counterparts just across the Bay Bridge in Oakland, California, do.

These patterns link up with another notable trend. Neighborhoods across the country have become more segregated by income over the past few decades. This has created isolated pockets of poverty and wealth where residents are mostly surrounded by people of the same economic class. ZIP code by ZIP code, county by county, and sometimes even block by block, Americans experience very different economic realities and chances for betterment. As the Economic Innovation Group, a bipartisan public policy organization, puts it, the result is "a deeply fragmented landscape of economic well-being—one in which far too many communities are being left behind."[3]

FACTORS THAT MATTER

What explains the variations in mobility rates across different areas of the country? Why is upward mobility so much higher in some areas than others? Chetty and other researchers at the Equality of Opportunity Project are trying to answer those questions. They looked at the patterns behind the geographical variation. They found several important factors that are correlated with mobility rates.

The first factor is economic segregation. Areas with a high concentration of poverty tend to have lower rates of intergenerational mobility. Conversely, neighborhoods with more economic diversity tend to have higher rates of intergenerational mobility. But the correlation is not explained at the individual level. In other words, the explanation of the effect is not that poor children have worse outcomes than wealthy children, and hence areas with more poor people have lower upward mobility.

GROWING APART

The gap between prosperous and poor ZIP codes is not only an income gap but also a growth gap. The United States' affluent neighborhoods have rebounded from the 2008 recession. On average, employment rose by almost 25 percent from 2011 to 2015 in prosperous ZIP codes. The number of business establishments grew by 12.6 percent. In contrast, on average, distressed ZIP codes lost 6 percent of their jobs from 2011 to 2015. The number of business establishments fell by 6.3 percent in these ZIP codes. Today, most of these ZIP codes have fewer jobs and businesses than they did in 2000.[4]

Instead, the correlation operates at the community level. In other words, the crucial factor is not an individual family's income, but the poverty of the community in which the family lives. Thus, poor children growing up in a mixed-income neighborhood have better outcomes than poor children who grow up in areas with a very high concentration of poverty.

The second factor is economic inequality. As noted previously, greater economic inequality is correlated with less upward mobility. The same correlation exists at the local level. Poor children growing up in areas where there are wide income gaps, with many people clustered at the extremes of the income distribution, have lower odds of being able to move up the economic ladder than children growing up in areas where incomes are more evenly clustered around the middle of the distribution. In other words, neighborhoods

More than 20 percent of children were living in rural poverty in 2016.

with more middle-class residents tend to have higher levels of upward mobility.

Social capital is the third factor in mobility rates. Social scientists use the term *social capital* to refer to the relationships and social networks that foster a sense of community belonging and shared trust in a local area. While it is difficult to quantify social capital, sociologists have identified several indicators that serve as measures of social capital and social ties, including census response rates, voter turnout, and participation in community organizations. Areas with more social capital, as measured by these factors, have greater rates of upward mobility than areas with less social capital.

The fourth factor is the quality of the K–12 educational system in a community. Measuring quality in terms of average test scores and dropout rates, researchers have found that children in neighborhoods with higher-quality public schools have better prospects for moving up the economic ladder

BOWLING ALONE

In his 2000 book, *Bowling Alone: The Collapse and Revival of American Community*, political theorist Robert Putnam argues that social capital has been declining in the United States since the 1950s. On average, Americans have become wealthier. However, at the same time they have become increasingly isolated and disengaged from their communities, with serious consequences for civic life. Putnam considers the changing bowling habits of Americans as an illustration. Although the popularity of bowling has increased, fewer Americans are joining bowling leagues.

Family structures can affect a child's class mobility.

than children in areas with poorly performing public schools.

Measures of family stability, such as the divorce rate and the fraction of children living in single-parent households, are highly correlated with mobility rates. In fact, the fraction of children living in single-parent households appears to be more strongly correlated with mobility than any of the other four factors. This variable also operates at the community level, rather than at the individual level. In other words, the idea is not that children with single parents have worse outcomes than children with two parents. Rather, areas with more single-parent families have significantly lower levels of upward mobility than areas with more two-parent families. Additionally, children of married parents have worse outcomes when they grow up in neighborhoods with many single-parent families.

UNEQUAL ZIP CODES

Like mobility rates, poverty and prosperity rates vary dramatically from place to place. Across the country, the gap between the rich and the poor is mapped as sharp divisions along neighborhood lines. For example, in Detroit, Michigan, almost one-half of children live in poverty. In the neighboring school district of Grosse Pointe, the child poverty level is significantly lower. Georgetown in Washington, DC, has a median household income of more than $136,000. In contrast, cash-strapped Anacostia in southeastern Washington, DC, has a median income of $25,106.[5] In a section of San Antonio, Texas, nearly one-half of adults have no high school diploma. More than one-half of the population is not working. And the median income is less than $20,000. By comparison, in San Antonio's wealthiest ZIP code, less than 3 percent of residents have no high school diploma. Less than one-third of the population is outside of the workforce. And the median income is $91,000.[6] This is well above the state median income of $55,653.[7]

And both children of single parents and children of married parents have higher rates of mobility in communities with fewer single parents.

GEOGRAPHY RULES

Recent research on mobility trends points to a key conclusion: the neighborhoods children grow up in have a profound effect on their outcomes in life. Factors such as labor market conditions, employment opportunities, and wages are clearly important to the economic well-being of Americans. But just as important are factors that shape children's lives long before they reach the age of employment, including the quality of schools, family structure, and the social environment.

Growing up in an area with less residential segregation, a larger middle class, more stable families, more social capital, and better public schools significantly increases one's prospects for upward mobility. But these are conditions that vary drastically across different regions and cities, and even from one block to the next. Thus, for many Americans, the odds of being able to move up in life come down to geography. As journalist Tanvi Misra puts it, "The American dream lives and dies at the local level."[8]

DISCUSSION STARTERS

- There are many characteristics of high-poverty neighborhoods that might explain why segregated poverty diminishes upward mobility. For example, low-income neighborhoods tend to have higher crime rates, lower-quality schools, poorer infrastructure, less access to amenities, and fewer job opportunities. In your view, which variables are most important?

- Were you surprised by any of the factors that are correlated with mobility? Why or why not?

- Why do you think that growing up in an area with a lot of single-parent households might diminish upward mobility even for children with married parents?

RACE
MATTERS

There are stark differences in upward mobility across geographical areas in the United States. But perhaps the nation's biggest opportunity gap is based on race. Politicians on both sides of the political aisle have argued that the United States doesn't have a race problem so much as it has a class problem. For example, in a 2013 speech on economic mobility, President Obama said that the opportunity gap is equally tied to class and race. Republican congressman Paul Mitchell, from Michigan's Tenth District, has argued that "the bigger struggle is a class warfare struggle, not a racial issue struggle. . . . It's about the haves and the have-nots."[1]

Yet research shows that African Americans are disproportionately represented at the bottom of the income

African Americans face a significant number of challenges when it comes to economic equality.

Studies show that African American men living below the poverty line have a higher risk for mortality compared with those who live above the poverty line.

scale. And in many cases, low-income African Americans face uniquely race-based obstacles to equality of opportunity that cannot simply be reduced to the disadvantages of class.

THE COLOR OF MONEY

African Americans have made great strides toward equality in many domains, including education, employment, and politics. However, when it comes to economic equality, the divide between black and white Americans remains deep.

African Americans are more than twice as likely as whites to be poor. Also, African Americans are vastly less likely than whites to make it to the top of the income distribution. In 2007, almost all of the top one percent of households by income were white, according to data from the Federal Reserve's Survey of Consumer Finances and the Tax Policy Center. Less than 2 percent were African American. The median net-asset worth of the top one percent of African American households was $1.2 million, compared with $8.3 million for white households.[2]

At every level of the income distribution, the median income of African Americans is lower than that of whites. And troublingly, African American households have seen their share of the economic pie decrease since 2000. African Americans are the only racial group in the United States making less now than they did in 2000. In 2000, the median household income of African Americans was $41,363. In 2016, it was just $39,490. By comparison, the median income for whites rose from $59,128 in 2000 to more than $65,000 in 2016.[3]

The pay gap persists even for college-educated African Americans. In fact, college-educated African Americans have seen their earnings decline the most in relation to those of their white counterparts. According to the Economic Policy Institute, college-educated African American males earned less than similarly educated white males in the 1980s. By 2014, the gap in incomes had doubled, with whites earning much more than blacks.

THE LATINO INCOME AND WEALTH GAP

African Americans face unique disadvantages because of the United States' legacy of slavery and segregation. However, American Latinos also lag behind whites in terms of income and wealth. The median household income for Latino households was $45,148 in 2016, or 30 percent less than that of whites.[5] And on average, Latino families have ten times less wealth than white families. The Institute for Policy Studies estimates that, at current rates, it would take Latino households 84 years to catch up their median wealth to that of white households.

THE RACIAL WEALTH GAP

For every $100 of income white families earn, African American families earn just $57.30. The wealth gap is even starker. For every $100 of wealth owned by white families, African American families own just $5.04.[4]

As with income, the wealth gap is widening. In 2010, the median household wealth of white families was eight times that of black families. By 2013, the median wealth of white households had jumped to 13 times the median wealth of black households, according to the Pew Research Center. This is the biggest it has been since 1989, when white households had 17 times the wealth of black households.[6]

African American wealth is declining not only in relation to that of whites but also in absolute terms. According to the Institute for Policy Studies, a progressive think tank, the median wealth of African American households fell by 75 percent from 1983 to 2013, dropping from $6,800 to $1,700. During the same period, the median white household saw a 14 percent increase in wealth, from $102,000 to $116,800.[7]

MIND THE GAP

The wealth gap between whites and blacks in the United States has far-reaching consequences for intergenerational mobility. Household wealth allows families to invest in opportunities—such as homeownership and education—that make it easier to climb up the economic ladder over time. In turn, wealth makes it easier to weather financial crises without slipping down the economic ladder when times get tough.

As sociologists Emily Beller and Michael Hout point out, "Without a cushion of inherited wealth, emergencies hit harder and people with no nest egg have to let opportunities pass by."[8] The result is a pattern of low upward mobility and high downward mobility that puts the American dream out of reach for many African Americans across the United States.

GETTING STUCK OR MOVING DOWN

African American children are not just more likely than white children to be born into families at the bottom of the economic ladder. They are also less likely to climb up the ladder as adults. According to the Pew Research Center, more than one-half of African American children born in the bottom income quintile remain stuck there as adults, compared with just one-third of whites.

And while poor African American families are more likely to stay poor than their white counterparts, middle-class African American families are more likely to fall down from the middle class than white families. More than one-half of African American children raised in the middle of the income distribution fall to the bottom two quintiles as adults. For whites, the number is much lower.

Similar patterns hold for wealth. Approximately one-half of African Americans raised at the bottom of the wealth distribution remain stuck at the bottom as adults. Just one-third of the lowest-income whites do. Sixty-eight percent of African Americans from the middle of the wealth ladder fall down to the bottom rungs, compared with 30 percent of middle-class whites.[9]

THE HOME AND NEIGHBORHOOD GAP

Discriminatory housing policies in the early and mid-1900s prevented many African Americans from buying homes. Today, there is still a significant homeownership gap between African Americans and whites. Less than one-half of African Americans own their own homes, compared with the majority of white Americans. There is also a notable racial divide when it comes to the neighborhoods where African American and white families live. The majority of young African Americans live in poor neighborhoods, compared with a significantly smaller portion of young whites. Across all income levels, almost one-half of African American families have lived in poor neighborhoods for at least two generations. For white families, the number is much lower.

A LEGACY OF DISCRIMINATION

Why is upward mobility so much lower for poor and middle-class African Americans than it is for their white counterparts? In large part, the unequal odds that African Americans face are the harmful legacy of discriminatory government policies. This discrimination forced African Americans into a position of disadvantage that still persists today.

The racially discriminatory federal housing policies of the early to mid-1900s are a prime example. These policies included restrictive housing covenants, the construction of segregated public housing projects, and redlining, which was the practice of refusing to approve mortgages based on race.

Established in 1934, the Federal Housing Administration (FHA) was created to regulate interest rates and mortgage terms after the Great Depression in the 1930s. The FHA home financing

Harlem in New York City is a well-known African American neighborhood.

system helped millions of white working-class Americans buy homes and gain a foothold in the middle class.

Yet the FHA refused to issue mortgages to African Americans. It also subsidized the building of subdivisions in suburbs across the United States. However, the FHA did this on the condition that the houses would not be sold to African Americans. As a result, African Americans were excluded from white middle-class suburbs and pushed into marginalized areas. This created patterns of residential segregation that are still in effect today.

White middle-class Americans, whose suburban homes have increased in value over the decades, gained a tremendous wealth advantage from home equity. Home equity is one of the main sources of wealth for middle-class Americans. In contrast, African American families were forced either to remain renters—thus gaining no equity at all—or to buy homes in less desirable neighborhoods, where their property accrued less value over time.

Predominantly African American neighborhoods faced discriminatory zoning policies. Industrial sites and sites for toxic waste disposal were more likely to be located in African American neighborhoods than in white ones. Discriminatory lending policies meant that African American home buyers were given unfavorable loan conditions compared with those given to their white counterparts. This meant African Americans had smaller savings and less disposable income than whites with similar incomes.

This government-sponsored discrimination created a wealth gap that has been passed on from generation to generation. Legal scholar Richard Rothstein noted that after the government applied those policies, economic inequality became a self-perpetuating cycle.

THE PAST IS PRESENT

In 1968, Congress passed the Fair Housing Act, which prohibited discrimination in housing. However, the law did nothing to reverse or remedy the effects of past discrimination, which created a system of unequal access to the wealth-generating opportunities that drive economic mobility for generations. By the time Congress acted, these inequalities had become deeply entrenched.

Today, the United States' past legacy of discrimination is compounded by racism that persists in the present. Although government-sponsored discrimination has been outlawed, African Americans continue to face prejudice on the job market, in the workplace, in the criminal justice system, and in many other spheres of life.

For example, African American prospective home buyers are shown fewer homes by real estate agents than white prospective buyers, according

GI INJUSTICE

The GI Bill was enacted in 1944 to help servicemen returning from World War II (1939–1945). The bill granted a number of benefits to veterans, ranging from college tuition assistance to low-cost home mortgages. Unlike the FHA, the Veterans Administration did not explicitly mandate racial discrimination in the provisions of the GI Bill. However, in practice, the GI Bill was applied in deeply discriminatory ways. For example, African American veterans were routinely denied the mortgage subsidies to which they were entitled. And many local benefits administrators refused to process African Americans' college applications. Instead, administrators steered African Americans into training for low-level jobs.

to a 2012 housing discrimination experiment. In the job market, African American applicants are much less likely to receive callbacks than similarly qualified white applicants. According to a National Bureau of Economic Research study, merely having a name that sounds stereotypically African American significantly reduces an applicant's chances of being hired.

At the same time, African American men are more likely to be arrested on drug charges than white men. This is despite the fact that white men are more likely than African American men to use or sell drugs. Once arrested, African American men are more likely than white men to be sentenced. And once they are

LESSONS FROM LEVITTOWN

In 1948, the homes in Levittown, New York, came with a price tag of approximately $8,000. Adjusting for inflation, that would be approximately $75,000 in today's dollars. This is an affordable price for many working-class families, both black and white. However, at the time, African Americans were not allowed to buy houses in Levittown. And by the time the Fair Housing Act was signed in 1968, abolishing housing discrimination, it was too late for many working-class African Americans. Housing prices shot up by 43 percent between 1970 and 1980. Meanwhile, wages for all Americans had begun to stagnate. African Americans in particular saw their median income drop by one percent over that period.

Today, Levittown houses sell for $350,000 and up. At six to seven times the median income, that puts them out of reach for most working-class Americans of either race. However, over three generations, the white working-class families who bought the houses in 1948—often with the help of low-cost mortgages denied to their African American counterparts—have gained more than $200,000 in the form of equity.[10]

sentenced, they are more likely to be given long jail terms. This cycle is just one symptom of the institutionalized racism found in the United States.

Discrimination in the criminal justice system leads to higher rates of incarceration for African Americans. The economic costs are great. Being convicted of a crime affects a person's employment prospects, earnings, and chances for economic mobility. It also takes a tremendous toll on one's children. Having a family member in prison leads to a loss of household income. It disrupts family stability. It also perpetuates a cycle of social marginalization.

DISCUSSION STARTERS

- What types of discriminatory practices toward minorities do you see or hear about today? How can you help stop discrimination?

- How might some of the general mobility trends help explain why African Americans have lower upward mobility rates than whites?

- What are some ways to reduce the wealth gap between blacks and whites?

SIX

EDUCATION: THE GREAT
EQUALIZER?

O ne way that racial disparities show themselves is in inequalities in education. The average white student attends a school scoring at the 60th percentile on standardized tests. In other words, average scores at these schools are higher than those of 60 percent of other test takers. By comparison, the average African American student attends a school that scores at the 37th percentile for tests. This gap extends to higher education also. Thirty-six percent of whites above the age of 25 have college degrees. Only 23 percent of similarly aged African Americans do.[1]

The race gap in education highlights a key fact about the state of education in the United States. Doing well in school

Even if white and African American children work just as hard in school, African American children are still more likely to be at a disadvantage.

is crucial to success. In particular, earning a college degree dramatically increases Americans' prospects for upward mobility. Yet the educational system all too often serves to reflect and replicate existing social disparities. This creates a vicious cycle. Socioeconomic inequalities and educational inequalities end up reinforcing each other. This is a problem that affects low-income students of all races, not just low-income African Americans.

AN UNEQUAL PLAYING FIELD

Students enter K–12 education with deep disparities in their backgrounds. These include differences in household income, access to quality early education programs, adequate nutrition and health care, exposure to books and academic enrichment at home, parental involvement, and the stability of the home and community environment. These disparities mean that children start off their lives from very different positions of advantage or disadvantage.

The ideal behind public education is to level the playing field. It is to provide students from all backgrounds with a quality education and an equal opportunity to succeed. Horace Mann, an educator and politician in the 1800s, called education the great equalizer because it is supposed to give everyone a fair and equal shot at getting ahead.

However, inequalities in children's backgrounds all too often translate into inequalities in schooling. Instead of leveling the playing field, schools can end up heightening the opportunity gap between better-off and worse-off students.

EDUCATIONAL ACHIEVEMENT GAP

Thanks to patterns of residential segregation, US public schools are highly segregated by economic status. Combined with the fact that schooling is financed largely at the local level, this means that there are significant gaps in quality between high-poverty and low-poverty schools. For example, high-poverty schools have a harder time attracting quality teachers. They also have a higher teacher turnover rate. Students at high-poverty schools have access to fewer resources and, in the course of a week, receive fewer hours of actual instruction time than students at low-poverty schools.

The result is that educational achievement often depends far too much on social class and income level. For example, family income is the best predictor of SAT scores. Students with household incomes of more than

QUALITY PAYS

How much impact can a quality teacher have on students' success? After examining school district and tax records for more than one million children, economists Raj Chetty, John Friedman, and Jonah Rockoff concluded that having a high-quality teacher—defined in terms of the teacher's impact on student test scores—increases the probability of college attendance. It also increases the quality of colleges that students attend, decreases the likelihood of teen pregnancy, and substantially boosts earnings. They found that having an above-average teacher can also raise a student's annual income.

Food Cabinet Donations

PLEASE DONATE NON-PERISHABLE FOODS ANYTIME
THANK YOU!

Greenleaf Kindness Connection

$200,000 score an average of 30 percent higher than students from families earning less than $20,000.[2] And high school students from families at the top of the income distribution are much more likely to enroll in college than students from families at the bottom of the pay ladder are. This gap is especially evident at the nation's most elite universities. Only approximately 3 percent of students at top colleges come from families in the bottom 25 percent of incomes. Approximately 74 percent of students come from the top 25 percent of incomes.[3]

PRICED OUT

Public schools are free, but parents who can afford it pay big bucks to live in high-achieving school districts. According to a Brookings Institution report, housing prices in the 100 largest metropolitan areas of the country are an average of 2.4 times more expensive for homes near high-scoring public schools, compared with homes near low-scoring schools. That comes out to an average difference in housing prices of $11,000 a year, putting top-quality schools out of reach for less-affluent parents.[4]

HIGH STAKES

To an increasing degree, today's economy depends on knowledge-based industries. This means that the importance of education has increased. Earning a college degree significantly increases prospects for upward mobility. Almost one-half of those raised in the lowest income rung remain stuck there as adults when they do not have a college degree. For those with a college degree, the number is much lower. And Americans with

four-year degrees are more likely than those without degrees to rise all the way from the bottom to the top of the income ladder.

Americans with college degrees also earn significantly more than Americans with only high school diplomas. On average, college graduates earn 56 percent more a year than those without college degrees.[5] This gap has almost tripled since 1980.

But because students from high-income families are more likely to go to college than students from low-income families, this wage gap creates a troubling dynamic. As the financial stakes of not going to college increase, the divide between those with college degrees and those without them widens. In turn, this widening economic divide further cements the achievement gap between rich and poor students.

LEFT BEHIND

After the 2008 recession, the recovering economy added millions of jobs. Of those jobs, the majority went to workers with at least some college education. This showed that Americans without college degrees were being left behind in the new economy. Yet a college degree is by no means a guaranteed ticket to success. In 2016, 5.6 percent of college graduates younger than 24 were unemployed. Approximately 12.6 percent were underemployed, or seeking full-time work but settling for part-time work. And 44.6 percent were working in lower-level jobs they were overqualified for.[7]

For low-income Americans, the result is a self-perpetuating cycle of downward mobility, with repercussions that last for generations.

As journalist Jason DeParle notes, "While in theory [the pay tilt toward educated workers] could help poor children rise— good learners can become high earners—more often it favors the children of the educated and affluent, who have access to better schools and arrive in them more prepared to learn."[6]

STEEP COSTS

Inequalities in K–12 education are one obstacle that can keep less-privileged Americans from moving up the economic ladder. Another is the rising cost of college tuition. Over the past two decades, the cost of a college degree has soared, far outpacing the cost of inflation. Tuition has increased at public universities and at private colleges. Meanwhile, median family incomes have stagnated. Adjusting for inflation, the incomes for many Americans have not increased at all over the past two decades.

For less-privileged students, this presents a dilemma. Without a college degree, it is hard to get ahead or even stay afloat. However, with less public financing of education, college is becoming more and more unaffordable. The average student debt for seniors graduating with loans exceeds $26,000. Almost 13 percent of student loan borrowers owe more than $50,000. Nearly 4 percent owe more than $100,000.[8]

Even for middle-class students, the burden of college debt is crushing. In some cases, the gains in income that come with a college degree may be canceled out by the crippling size of student loan payments. Living paycheck to paycheck without

ALL IN THE FAMILY

In the United States, there is a significant correlation between parents' income and their children's income as adults. A recent study by economists Joseph Ferrie, Catherine Massey, and Jonathan Rothbaum looked at educational outcomes specifically. They found that the correlation in educational attainment between parents and children is even higher than the correlation in income. Taking into account data from both parents and grandparents to get a more long-term picture of patterns across generations, Ferrie and his colleagues calculated an educational elasticity score as high as 0.7.[9] Roughly, this means that for every extra year of schooling parents have, their children will end up with approximately seven-tenths of a year of schooling more than someone whose parents have less schooling. In other words, how much education parents get highly determines their children's own educational attainment.

Andrew Cuomo is the governor of New York. He supported a bill to give poor and middle-class students free tuition at New York public colleges. The program is called the Excelsior Scholarship.

being able to accumulate the savings necessary for financial security, an increasing number of college graduates are just one unforeseen emergency away from slipping down the economic ladder.

This problem will only get worse. As the number of Americans going to college has increased, the return on the investment has decreased. This has resulted in credentials inflation. An undergraduate degree means less than it used to. Increasingly, students now need a graduate degree to get ahead. This can mean taking on even more student debt.

DISCUSSION STARTERS

- One problem that high-poverty schools in the United States face is that they are much less likely to attract top-notch teachers. What could be done in the United States to attract higher-quality teachers to disadvantaged schools?

- Harvard University's Ronald Ferguson noted that inequalities in education are the source of greater inequalities. Do you agree? Why or why not?

- Some people argue that the cost of a college degree may not be worth it for some people. Do you agree or disagree?

SEVEN

CLOSING
THE GAP

E conomic mobility is a bipartisan issue. Both Democrats
and Republicans agree that upward mobility is the crux of
the American dream and that diminishing opportunities
for advancement are a cause for concern. President Obama
has called growing inequality and a lack of upward mobility a
challenge of our current era. Across the political aisle, Republican
senator Marco Rubio from Florida has said that if the United
States wants to stay remarkable, the country needs to close the
opportunity gap. But while both political parties agree on the
importance of mobility, there is little bipartisan agreement on
what to do about it. This makes it difficult to find solutions both
parties can support.

Senator Elizabeth Warren has expressed concern
about class mobility in the United States.

A DIVIDE

Democrats tend to favor using the government to help the poor and reduce the income gap. This includes investing more money in education, job training, family leave policies, and government programs to strengthen the social safety net. It also includes supporting policies that put more economic rewards in the hands of middle-class and lower-income Americans. These policies include raising the minimum wage, revising the tax code to benefit low- and middle-income Americans, instituting more corporate regulations to protect consumers, and reducing the college debt burden on students. The goal is to help correct a skewed system of advantages that disproportionately benefits the wealthiest while also growing the economy by strengthening the middle class.

Republicans tend to be less committed to government solutions to poverty and inequality. Many Republicans see government involvement as a barrier to mobility. Instead, they advocate for reducing

TAKING LEAVE

Democratic senator from New York Kirsten Gillibrand introduced a bill for universal paid family leave in 2012. Her bill promises up to 12 weeks of paid time off for any worker. Currently, only a small number of US workers have access to paid family leave. At the start of 2018, the bill had not passed. The United States is the only developed nation that doesn't guarantee paid leave to all workers if they have a child, get sick, or need to take time off work to care for a family member. Without a paid leave policy, workers may be forced to quit after a family emergency or a birth. This hurts both families and the economy.

regulations on businesses, cutting spending, and lowering taxes on corporate profits and investments. In their view, this will stimulate the economy and in turn create more opportunities for all Americans.

In place of government initiatives, Republicans prefer to focus on family, community, and personal values such as self-reliance, responsibility, and hard work. For example, they emphasize the importance of strengthening marriage as an institution to make families more stable. And they think that civic and religious organizations are in a better position than the government to help individuals. As a House Republican policy paper put it, "No amount of government intervention can replace the great drivers of American life: our families, friends, neighbors, churches, and charities."[1]

TAX TROUBLE

A progressive tax system takes a larger percentage from higher-income earners than it does from lower-income individuals. This is a way to benefit lower-wage earners and also to stimulate the economy, given lower-wage earners' higher marginal rate of consumption. Over the past few decades, the United States' system has become less progressive. The top one percent of Americans have seen their average federal taxes decrease, while the middle-class tax burden has remained fairly constant. In addition, there are many special provisions in the tax code that disproportionately benefit high earners. Examples include tax deductions for vacation homes and lower tax rates for investments.

Nutrition programs at schools give students access to healthy food.

BRIDGING THE DIVIDE

The causes of declining mobility are complex, involving a constellation of different factors interacting on different levels. Just as the problem is complex, so too should be the approach to solving it. Both the Democratic and the Republican perspectives have a role to play.

Family stability and social capital have a significant influence on children's prospects for success. In this regard, community-based programs that create partnerships between schools, families, and civic organizations can be extremely effective. These include initiatives to provide parenting education and offer support services through local agencies. Community networks that mentor students throughout their schooling are another example. Such programs align with the

Republican focus on strong families, community building, civic values, and local solutions.

However, weakened families and fraying social ties are often symptoms of deeper underlying causes. Poverty, unemployment, educational inequalities, high rates of incarceration, and unequal access to resources can take a toll on families. Stagnating wages and poor economic growth can decimate communities. To address these deeper, systemic problems, people need solutions at the level of government policy. This aligns with the Democratic focus on investing in programs to help low-income and middle-class Americans.

Investing in education—especially early education—and vocational training can have the most impact on lower-income Americans. Improving access to social resources, such as health care, is also vital.

IN SICKNESS AND IN HEALTH

The United States has worse health outcomes, including higher rates of infant mortality and shorter life expectancy, than other developed nations. One reason is that the United States has more poverty and less-generous social welfare programs than other advanced countries. Another reason is that access to health care is very uneven. The United States is the only advanced nation without universal health-care coverage. This means that many of the poorest Americans are not able to afford proper care, including preventative care.

Unequal access to health care is not only a fairness issue. It is also a class mobility issue. This is because of the relationship between health inequality and economic inequality. Income level affects health. Low-income Americans are more likely to have poor health outcomes. But, in turn, health affects income level. Health problems can limit education and employment opportunities. As a result, health inequality can limit many Americans' future prospects for success.

SPENDING BACKWARD

Research shows that government spending on social services boosts upward mobility and improves equality of opportunity. However, as Chetty notes, sometimes the solution isn't to spend more. Instead, what people need to do is to spend money in a smarter, more efficient way.

For example, consider education expenditures. Currently, the United States spends more on education than any other developed nation. However, the bulk of this spending goes to tertiary education, meaning college and other postsecondary education. Given that lower-income Americans are significantly less likely to attend college, this educational spending ends up disproportionately benefiting the already relatively well-off.

American citizens and politicians have had heated debates about the Affordable Care Act, which led to broader health insurance coverage.

To have a greater effect on less privileged students, resources could be allocated in the opposite way. There could be more investment in early childhood education and in improving quality at the K–12 level. In particular, more resources could be allocated to students from disadvantaged backgrounds specifically.

Instead, as an OECD report noted, the United States is actually one of only three OECD nations that spend less, on average, on lower-income students than on other students. The result is that the US education system is less effective at

GETTING AN EARLY START

One of the most promising ways to invest in education is to institute universal early education. This includes free, quality preschool education for children under age four. Early education helps equalize educational outcomes for children from disadvantaged backgrounds. It can also improve parents' finances by lessening the cost of childcare and preschool. Because high-quality childcare and private preschools are so expensive, many parents are forced to settle for lower-quality programs. This starts their children off at a disadvantage compared with children whose families are able to afford better options. Some families opt to have a parent stay home as the caretaker instead of working. These years outside the workforce can make it difficult to find good job opportunities in the future. This takes a toll on family earnings. Interestingly, early childhood education is one policy area that has strong bipartisan support. According to a 2016 First Five Years Fund poll, the majority of supporters of Republican president Donald Trump favored making early childhood education more available and affordable. The majority of supporters for former Democratic presidential candidate Hillary Clinton felt the same way.

helping children from all socioeconomic backgrounds realize their potential.

SKEWED PRIORITIES

A similar pattern holds for other areas of government spending. For example, the federal government spends almost three times more on homeownership subsidies than it does on rental assistance. And more than one-half of those subsidies benefit high-income households earning more than $100,000 per year. In the meantime, more than 75 percent of all renters in the United States spend a higher portion of their income on rent than the threshold commonly defined as affordable.[2]

In general, the United States spends approximately 1.6 percent of its GDP each year on government assistance programs. Yet only 25 percent of this spending goes toward helping lower- and middle-income Americans.[3] From how the tax code works to how benefits are distributed, the system is disproportionately skewed toward the interests of the better-off. Closing the opportunity gap and reviving the American dream for low-income Americans will take a new generation of policies—from both sides of the political aisle.

DISCUSSION STARTERS

- What types of policies do you think can have the biggest effect on upward mobility and economic opportunity?

- What kinds of tax reforms do you think may have an impact on upward mobility?

- Over the past few decades, Americans have become increasingly divided along political party lines. This makes it difficult to find shared solutions to important problems. Why do you think that Americans have become so divided? What can we do about it?

RECENT TRENDS, FUTURE CHALLENGES

T he United States' opportunity gap has increasingly been at the forefront of public debate over the past few years. This is in large part thanks to movements such as Occupy Wall Street. This grassroots movement emerged in 2011 to protest income inequality, corporate greed, and the corrupting influence of money on politics. The movement's slogan, "We are the 99 percent," has become a catchphrase for describing the state of inequality in the United States.[1]

Grassroots movements like Occupy Wall Street have helped inspire initiatives in the political arena to address inequality. Several cities and states have voted to increase their minimum wages, including Alaska, Arkansas, Connecticut, Nebraska, New Jersey, New York, South Dakota, and Washington, DC.

The Occupy Wall Street movement encouraged people to take action against economic injustices.

THE OCCUPY MOVEMENT

The Occupy Wall Street movement started out modestly. On September 17, 2011, demonstrators marched through Wall Street toward the New York Stock Exchange, protesting economic inequality and corporate influence on politics. That night, protesters pitched tents and camped in Zuccotti Park, in the heart of New York City's financial district. Every day for weeks, more tents showed up. By October, the plaza had turned into a vast tent city, with hundreds of protesters occupying the space. The Zuccotti Park occupation lasted for one month and 29 days. On November 15, New York City police evicted the protesters and cleared the park. However, by then Occupy Wall Street had grown into a national movement. Occupations sprang up across the country. Tens of thousands of demonstrators took to the streets in New York and in other major cities. And the movement succeeded in drawing national attention to the United States' growing economic divide, inspiring other grassroots efforts, such as the "Fight for 15" campaign to raise the minimum wage.

On the federal level, Senator Elizabeth Warren, a Democrat from Massachusetts, has made standing up to Wall Street a central theme of her political career. Since being elected in 2012, she has supported many efforts to strengthen financial regulations and to address income inequality. This includes the Bank on Students Emergency Loan Refinancing Act, which would allow students to refinance college loans at a lower federal rate. In May 2017, Senate Democrats introduced legislation to raise the federal minimum wage to $15 an hour by 2024. And in February 2017, Senators Tim Scott, a Republican from South Carolina, and Cory Booker, a Democrat from New Jersey, introduced the bipartisan Investing in Opportunity Act. Its goal is to help revitalize economically distressed communities by promoting investment and new businesses.

THE 2016 PRESIDENTIAL ELECTION

Issues of economic inequality and mobility also played an important role in the 2016 presidential election. Many pundits have claimed that the economic anxiety of working-class voters propelled President Donald Trump to his surprise electoral win. The data do not actually support this interpretation. In fact, presidential candidate Hillary Clinton led among voters with incomes below the median. By contrast, the majority of Trump voters came from the top one-half of the income distribution, including the most affluent portions of the distribution.

Although the media stereotype of the economically anxious Trump voter doesn't hold up, issues of economic inequality and mobility were defining themes of the campaign in other ways. As the Democratic nominee, Clinton put together what is considered the party's most progressive platform to date on social and

THE COST OF FREE

In April 2017, New York became the first state to implement a plan to make in-state public universities tuition-free for families earning up to $125,000.[2] However, some critics argue that the plan benefits middle-class students more than low-income students. The scholarship covers financial needs not met by other forms of financial aid, such as Federal Pell Grants. This means that low-income students get less money out of the program than students from families too wealthy to qualify for federal aid. Also, the scholarship does not cover university fees or room and board, which are significant costs for low-income students.

Donald Trump and Hillary Clinton had heated debates during the 2016 presidential campaign.

economic issues. The platform included plans for universal early education, paid family leave, expanded health-care access, and job creation programs. And in different ways, both Trump and Bernie Sanders, Clinton's challenger during the Democratic primary, ran on economically populist messages, presenting themselves as fighting against the powerful interests of establishment elites.

Sanders, an Independent senator from Vermont, entered the race for the Democratic nomination with a speech declaring, "This campaign is going to send a message to the billionaire class."[3] His signature issues were income inequality, financial reform, tuition-free college, and single-payer health care.

Trump launched his bid for the presidency with a speech in which he declared that the "American dream is dead" and campaigned on the slogan "Make America Great Again."[4] He pledged to revitalize small towns, invest in infrastructure, bring back manufacturing jobs, and protect US workers from unfair trade agreements.

THE WILL FOR CHANGE

Whatever role economic anxiety played in the 2016 election, many Americans are clearly concerned about growing inequality. According to a 2015 *New York Times*/CBS News poll, most Americans thought that the government needed to do more to decrease the gap between the rich and the poor. The majority favored raising taxes on those making more than $1 million a year. The majority were also in favor of raising the minimum wage. And they thought that employers should guarantee paid family leave for employees needing to take time off to care for a child or other family member.

Increasing opportunity and mobility for all Americans involves tackling many challenges. Many interacting forces have shaped the current

THE LAST EMBERS OF AN INDUSTRY

Trump campaigned on the promise of bringing back jobs in the coal industry. As president, he doubled down on that promise, vowing to lift environmental restrictions that he blamed for the industry's decline. Critics argue that technological change, not environmental regulations, has killed the industry. Instead of futile promises to revive a dying industry, critics argue, it makes more sense to invest in the new technologies of the future and to provide US workers with the training they need to get good jobs in these fields.

state of opportunity in the United States. Trade, globalization, and technology have affected the jobs and wages that are available to Americans. Entrenched racial inequalities have worsened the disadvantages of class for low-income Americans of color. Shrinking unions have left many workers in a weaker bargaining position. Deregulation of corporations and tax policies that benefit the wealthiest have tipped the scales in favor of the top one percent of Americans.

THE FUTURE OF WORK

There are also emerging trends creating new obstacles to upward mobility. One is that companies are increasingly shifting to a contractor model of employment. In this model, companies hire fewer permanent, full-time staff. They rely more on independent contractors, or outside workers, to perform

Contract workers have less job security than full-time employees.

jobs. This allows corporations to cut costs and increase profits. However, many experts think that this shift to hiring contract workers contributes to declining mobility and rising inequality in the United States. The companies that supply contract employees compete by lowering costs. This drives wages down. On top of this, employees who work on a contract basis have fewer opportunities for career advancement. And compared with permanent, full-time employees, independent contractors typically receive fewer, if any, job benefits. These include paid vacation time, sick leave, health insurance coverage, and training and education benefits.

Another trend that could have even bigger consequences for workers in the United States is the automation of jobs. As technology improves, an increasing number of jobs are being automated, or performed by robots, machines, or computer programs. Experts predict that this has the potential to put millions of people out of work. Jobs involving repetitive and routine tasks are the most at risk. These include jobs in

DRIVING THE FUTURE

In October 2016, an 18-wheeler loaded with 2,000 cases of beer drove approximately 120 miles (193 km) from Fort Collins, Colorado, to Colorado Springs. The catch? There was no driver at the wheel. This was the first commercial delivery made by a driverless truck. It was the brainchild of Otto, a start-up company funded by the ridesharing company Uber. Otto specializes in self-driving vehicles. This technology is set to transform the future of driving. It could also hit many workers hard. Experts predict that up to five million US jobs could be lost.[5]

construction, transportation, and manufacturing, as well as many office jobs, such as accounting and clerical work. In a survey conducted by Yale and Oxford researchers, experts estimated that such routine jobs could disappear by the mid-2030s.

THE PRICE OF INACTION

These and other challenges will be difficult to address. However, the costs of growing inequality are too great to ignore. The price of inaction is too high. Economic inequality seeps into other arenas of life, creating inequalities on many different levels, from unequal access to decent health care and quality education, to disparities in rates of incarceration. Because money buys access, economic inequality also leads to inequality of political power. Some people end up having less of a voice. This distorts the democratic process. It also endangers the ideal of equal opportunity and upward mobility—the promise at the heart of the American dream.

DISCUSSION STARTERS

- What can you do to pressure politicians to help people achieve upward class mobility?

- Do any forces that prevent class mobility affect your life? If so, what can you or your local government do to change this?

- What can movements such as Occupy Wall Street do to create change in class mobility?

ESSENTIAL FACTS

SIGNIFICANT EVENTS

- The Occupy Wall Street movement began in 2011 when thousands of demonstrators marched on Wall Street toward the New York Stock Exchange in New York City. The movement quickly gained momentum, and thousands more joined the cause. The movement's goal was to protest corporate greed, income inequality, and the corrupting influence of money on politics.

- In 2015, approximately 60,000 low-wage workers protested for better working conditions, a higher minimum wage, and the ability to form unions. The protest wanted to make people aware of the economic inequalities in the United States, which make class mobility difficult.

- Issues of economic inequality played a big role in the 2016 presidential election. Donald Trump told the public that he would invest in infrastructure, revitalize small towns, protect US workers from unfair trade agreements, and bring back manufacturing jobs. Hillary Clinton put together plans for universal early education, paid family leave, expanded health-care access, and job creation. Bernie Sanders's signature issues were income inequality, financial reform, tuition-free college, and single-payer health care.

KEY PLAYERS

- Historian James Truslow Adams originated the term *American dream*, which refers to the idea that individuals should have equal opportunities to get ahead based on hard work. Having the chance to become upwardly mobile is a key component of this.

- Italian sociologist and statistician Corrado Gini developed the Gini coefficient, which is a way to measure economic inequality.

- Alan Krueger, a Princeton economist who served as chair of the Council of Economic Advisors in the Obama administration, coined the term *Great Gatsby Curve* to describe the correlation between economic inequality and social mobility. He noticed the correlation in data collected by Miles Corak, a professor of economics at Ottawa University.

- Stanford University economist Raj Chetty collaborated with other researchers at the Equality of Opportunity Project to study class mobility in the United States.

IMPACT ON SOCIETY

Movement from one economic class to another has stalled in the United States during the past few decades. Despite its reputation as the land of opportunity, the United States lags behind other comparably advanced nations in terms of upward mobility and equality of opportunity. In addition to the constraints of class that limit the opportunities of low-income Americans of all races, African Americans face uniquely race-based obstacles to equality of opportunity. As a result, upward mobility is lower for African Americans. Increasing Americans' prospects for upward mobility requires a bipartisan commitment to improving lower-income Americans' access to quality education and other social resources, such as health care, job training, and affordable housing.

QUOTE

"We are forcing a real conversation about how to solve the grossest inequality in our generation. People are sick of wealth at the top and no accountability for corporations."

—*Mary Kay Henry, international president of the Service Employees International Union*

GLOSSARY

ASSET
An item of value.

BIPARTISAN
Involving cooperation between the two major political parties.

DISPARITY
A great difference.

DISPROPORTIONATE
Out of proportion in size, number, or effect; too large or too small in comparison with what would be expected or justified.

GDP
Gross domestic product, the monetary value of all goods and services produced within a nation's geographic borders over a specified period of time.

HOUSING COVENANT
A contractual agreement that governs the terms of the sale or lease of property.

INCARCERATION
The act of putting someone in prison or jail.

INTERGENERATIONAL INCOME ELASTICITY
A measure of the effect of parents' income status on that of their children.

MERITOCRATIC
Characterizing a system in which people are rewarded based on merit, not on class privilege.

PUNDIT
A person who gives opinions and commentary through the mass media.

STAGNATE
To cease to move or change.

SUBDIVISION
A large piece of land divided into smaller lots for the purpose of selling them so that homes can be built on them.

SUBSIDIZE
To pay part of the cost of something in order to lower the price for the purchaser.

ADDITIONAL
RESOURCES

SELECTED BIBLIOGRAPHY

Chetty, Raj, et al. "The Fading American Dream: Trends in Absolute Income Mobility Since 1940." *Science* 356.6336 (2017): 398–406. Print.

Putnam, Robert D. *Our Kids: The American Dream in Crisis*. New York: Simon, 2015. Print.

Rothstein, Richard. *The Color of Law: A Forgotten History of How Our Government Segregated America*. New York: Liveright, 2017. Print.

FURTHER READINGS

Eboch, M. M. *Race and Economics*. Minneapolis: Abdo, 2018. Print.

Merino, Noël, ed. *Income Inequality*. Farmington Hills, MI: Greenhaven, 2016. Print.

Thompson, Laurie Ann. *Be a Changemaker: How to Start Something That Matters*. New York: Simon Pulse, 2014. Print.

ONLINE RESOURCES

Booklinks
NONFICTION NETWORK
FREE! ONLINE NONFICTION RESOURCES

To learn more about class mobility, visit **abdobooklinks.com**. These links are routinely monitored and updated to provide the most current information available.

MORE INFORMATION

For more information on this subject, contact or visit the following organizations:

AMERICA'S PROMISE ALLIANCE
1110 Vermont Avenue NW, #900
Washington, DC 20005
202-657-0600
americaspromise.org

An alliance of nonprofit community organizations, businesses, and government organizations, America's Promise Alliance is dedicated to improving children's outcomes and increasing educational opportunities.

PROSPERITY NOW
1200 G Street NW, #400
Washington, DC 20005
202-408-9788
prosperitynow.org

Prosperity Now combines research, advocacy work, and community development to tackle economic inequality and promote financial security for low-income families in the United States.

UNITED FOR A FAIR ECONOMY
62 Summer Street
Boston, MA 02110
617-423-2148
faireconomy.org

United for a Fair Economy, a nonpartisan, nonprofit organization with a focus on tax- and budget-related issues, is dedicated to achieving greater economic equality and highlighting the dangers of the United States' wealth gap.

SOURCE NOTES

CHAPTER 1. A DIVIDED NATION

1. Steven Greenhouse and Jana Kasperkevic. "Fight for $15 Swells into Largest Protest by Low-Wage Workers in US history." *Guardian*. Guardian News and Media Limited, 15 Apr. 2015. Web. 4 Jan. 2018.

2. Greenhouse and Kasperkevic, "Fight for $15 Swells into Largest Protest by Low-Wage Workers in US history."

3. Yang Jiang, et al. "Basic Facts about Low-Income Children." *National Center for Children in Poverty*. Columbia University, Feb. 2016. Web. 4 Jan. 2018.

4. Kenan Fikri and John Lettieri. "The 2017 Distressed Communities Index." *Economic Innovation Group*. Economic Innovation Group, n.d. Web. 4 Jan. 2018.

5. Emmanuel Saez and Gabriel Zucman. "Wealth Inequality in the United States Since 1913: Evidence from Capitalized Income Tax Data." *Econometrics Laboratory*. University of California, Berkeley, May 2016. Web. 4 Jan. 2018.

6. Noah Kirsch. "The 5 Richest Americans Are Already $67 Billion Richer in 2017." *Forbes*. Forbes Media, 29 July 2017. Web. 4 Jan. 2018.

7. Patricia Cohen. "A Bigger Economic Pie, but a Smaller Slice for Half of the US." *New York Times*. New York Times Company, 6 Dec. 2016. Web. 4 Jan. 2018.

8. Thomas Piketty. *Capital in the Twenty-First Century*. Cambridge, MA: Harvard UP, 2014. Print. 332.

9. Ron Haskins. *Creating an Opportunity Society*. Washington, DC: Brookings Institution, 2009. Print. 8.

10. Kristen Doerer. "CEO Pay Down—to 'Only' 271 Times That of the Typical Worker." *PBS News Hour*. NewsHour Productions, 28 July 2017. Web. 4 Jan. 2018.

11. Chuck Collins and Josh Hoxie. "Billionaire Bonanza: The Forbes 400 and the Rest of Us." *Institute for Policy Studies*. Institute for Policy Studies, 1 Dec. 2015. Web. 4 Jan. 2018.

12. Josh Harkinson. "Chart: 6 Walmart Heirs Hold More Wealth Than 42% of Americans Combined." *Mother Jones*. Mother Jones, 18 July 2012. Web. 4 Jan. 2018.

13. "Tackling High Inequality, Creating Opportunity for All." *OECD*. Organisation for Economic Cooperation and Development, June 2014. Web. 4 Jan. 2018.

14. Joseph Stiglitz. *The Great Divide*. New York: Norton, 2015. Print. 88.

15. Stiglitz, *The Great Divide*, 179.

16. Michael Specter. "Life-Expectancy Inequality Grows in America." *New Yorker*. Condé Nast, 16 Apr. 2016. Web. 4 Jan. 2018.

17. David Cay Johnston. "Richest Are Leaving Even the Rich Far Behind." *New York Times*. New York Times Company, 5 June 2005. Web. 4 Jan. 2018.

18. "Federal Poverty Level (FPL)." *HealthCare.gov*. US Centers for Medicare & Medicaid Services, n.d. Web. 4 Jan. 2018.

19. Jessica L. Semega, et al. "Income and Poverty in the United States: 2016." *United States Census Bureau*. US Department of Commerce, 12 Sept. 2017. Web. 4 Jan. 2018.

20. "What Is Deep Poverty?" *Center for Poverty Research*. UC Davis Center for Poverty Research, n.d. Web. 4 Jan. 2018.

21. "Income Inequality and Poverty Rising in Most OECD Countries." *OECD*. Organisation for Economic Cooperation and Development, 21 Oct. 2008. Web. 4 Jan. 2018.

22. Barack Obama. "Remarks by the President on Economic Mobility." *White House*. White House, 4 Dec. 2013. Web. 4 Jan. 2018.

CHAPTER 2. CLASS CONSTRAINTS AND CLASS MOBILITY

1. Marjorie Connelly. "The Poll Results." *New York Times*. New York Times Company, 15 May 2005. Web. 4 Jan. 2018.

2. Paul Ryan. "Saving the American Idea: Rejecting Fear, Envy, and the Politics of Division." *Heritage Foundation*. Heritage Foundation, 15 Nov. 2011. Web. 4 Jan. 2018.

3. Julia B. Isaacs. "International Comparisons of Economic Mobility." *Brookings*. Brookings Institution, n.d. Web. 4 Jan. 2018.

4. Joe Pinsker. "America Is Even Less Socially Mobile Than Most Economists Thought." *Atlantic*. Atlantic Monthly Group, 23 July 2015. Web. 4 Jan. 2018.

5. "A Family Affair: Intergenerational Social Mobility across OECD Countries." *OECD*. Organisation for Economic Cooperation and Development, n.d. Web. 4 Jan. 2018.

6. Miles Corak. "Inequality from Generation to Generation: The United States in Comparison." *IZA Discussion Papers* 9929 (2012): 2. Print.

7. Jason DeParle. "Harder for Americans to Rise from Lower Rungs." *New York Times*. New York Times Company, 4 Jan. 2012. Web. 4 Jan. 2018.

8. Ron Haskins. *Creating an Opportunity Society*. Washington, DC: Brookings Institution, 2009. Print. 66.

9. DeParle, "Harder for Americans to Rise from Lower Rungs."

10. Reihan Salam. "Should We Care about Relative Mobility?" *National Review*. National Review, 28 Nov. 2011. Web. 4 Jan. 2018.

11. Neil Gilbert. "Prosperity, Not Upward Mobility, Is What Matters." *Atlantic*. Atlantic Monthly Group, 5 Jan. 2017. Web. 4 Jan. 2018.

12. Alex Bell, et al. "Who Becomes an Inventor in America? The Importance of Exposure to Innovation." *Equality of Opportunity Project*. Equality of Opportunity Project, n.d. Web. 4 Jan. 2018.

13. Bell, et al, "Who Becomes an Inventor in America?"

CHAPTER 3. INEQUALITY AND UPWARD MOBILITY

1. Robert J. Gordon. "American Growth Has Slowed Down. Get Used to It." *Politico Magazine*. Politico, n.d. Web. 5 Jan. 2018.

2. Christopher Ingraham. "The Richest 1 Percent Now Owns More of the Country's Wealth Than at Any Time in the Past 50 Years." *Washington Post*. Washington Post, 6 Dec. 2017. Web. 4 Jan. 2018.

3. Kathrin Brandmeir, et al. "Allianz Global Wealth Report 2016." *Allianz*. Allianz, n.d. Web. 5 Jan. 2018.

4. "OECD Income Distribution Database (IDD): Gini, Poverty, Income, Methods and Concepts." *OECD*. Organisation for Economic Cooperation and Development, n.d. Web. 5 Jan. 2018.

5. Era Dabla-Norris, et al. "Causes and Consequences of Income Inequality: A Global Perspective." *International Monetary Fund*. International Monetary Fund, 15 June 2015. Web. 4 Jan. 2018.

6. "Inequality Hurts Economic Growth, Finds OECD Research." *OECD*. Organisation for Economic Cooperation and Development, n.d. Web. 5 Jan. 2018.

7. Megan Thompson. "Buffett: People Living in Poverty Suffer from the 'American Nightmare.'" *PBS News Hour*. NewsHour Productions, 9 May 2015. Web. 5 Jan. 2018.

CHAPTER 4. THE GEOGRAPHY OF MOBILITY

1. Raj Chetty, et al. "Where Is the Land of Opportunity? The Geography of Intergenerational Mobility in the United States." *National Bureau of Economic Research*. National Bureau of Economic Research, Jan. 2014. Web. 5 Jan. 2018.

2. Stephen J. Dubner. "Is the American Dream Really Dead?" *Freakonomics*. Freakonomics, 18 Jan. 2017. Web. 5 Jan. 2018.

3. Kenan Fikri and John Lettieri. "The 2017 Distressed Communities Index" *Economic Innovation Group*. Economic Innovation Group, n.d. Web. 5 Jan. 2018.

4. Fikri and Lettieri, "The 2017 Distressed Communities Index."

5. "Georgetown (Hillandale) Neighborhood in Washington, District of Columbia (DC), 20007, 20057 Detailed Profile." *City-Data.com*. Advameg, n.d. Web. 5 Jan. 2018.

6. "78258 Zip Code Map & Detailed Profile." *Zip Atlas*. ZipAtlas.com, n.d. Web. 5 Jan. 2018.

SOURCE NOTES
CONTINUED

7. "Texas Household Income." *Department of Numbers*. Department of Numbers, n.d. Web. 5 Jan. 2018.

8. Tanvi Misra. "Where the American Dream Lives and Dies." *CityLab*. Atlantic Monthly Group, 23 Mar. 2017. Web. 5 Jan. 2018.

CHAPTER 5. RACE MATTERS

1. Daniel Allott. "Republican Congressman: Class, Not Race, Is the Dominant Struggle of Our Political Age." *Washington Examiner*. Washington Examiner, 11 Oct. 2017. Web. 5 Jan. 2018.

2. Antonio Moore. "America's Financial Divide: The Racial Breakdown of US Wealth in Black and White." *Huffpost*. Oath, 13 Apr. 2015. Web. 5 Jan. 2018.

3. Heather Long. "African Americans Are the Only Racial Group in US Still Making Less Than They Did in 2000." *Washington Post*. Washington Post, 15 Sept. 2017. Web. 5 Jan. 2018.

4. Emily Badger. "Whites Have Huge Wealth Edge over Blacks (But Don't Know It)." *New York Times*. New York Times Company, 18 Sept. 2017. Web. 5 Jan. 2018.

5. Jens Manuel Krogstad and Antonio Flores. "Latinos Made Economic Strides in 2015 after Years of Few Gains." *Pew Research Center*. Pew Research Center, 21 Nov. 2016. Web. 5 Jan. 2018.

6. Rakesh Kochhar and Richard Fry. "Wealth Inequality Has Widened along Racial, Ethnic Lines Since End of Great Recession." *Pew Research Center*. Pew Research Center, 12 Dec. 2014. Web. 5 Jan. 2018.

7. Dedrick Asante-Muhammad, et al. "The Road to Zero Wealth." *Institute for Policy Studies*. Institute for Policy Studies, Sept. 2017. Web. 5 Jan. 2018.

8. Emily Beller and Michael Hout. "Intergenerational Social Mobility: The United States in Comparative Perspective." *The Future of Children* (2006): 26. Print.

9. Susan K. Urahn, et al. "Pursuing the American Dream: Economic Mobility across Generations." *Pew Charitable Trusts*. Pew Charitable Trusts, July 2012. Web. 5 Jan. 2018.

10. Richard Rothstein. *The Color of Law*. New York: Liveright, 2017. Print. 181–182.

CHAPTER 6. EDUCATION: THE GREAT EQUALIZER?

1. "On Views of Race and Inequality, Blacks and Whites Are Worlds Apart." *Pew Research Center*. Pew Research Center, 27 June 2016. Web. 5 Jan. 2018.

2. Zachary A. Goldfarb. "These Four Charts Show How the SAT Favors Rich, Educated Families." *Washington Post*. Washington Post, 5 Mar. 2014. Web. 5 Jan. 2018.

3. Allan Ornstein. *Class Counts: Education, Inequality, and the Shrinking Middle Class*. Lanham, MD: Rowman, 2007. Print. VII.

4. Jonathan Rothwell. "Housing Costs, Zoning, and Access to High-Scoring Schools." *Brookings*. Brookings Institution, 19 Apr. 2012. Web. 5 Jan. 2018.

5. Christopher S. Rugaber. "Pay Gap between College Grads and Everyone Else at a Record." *USA Today*. USA Today, 12 Jan. 2017. Web. 5 Jan. 2018.

6. Jason DeParle. "Harder for Americans to Rise from Lower Rungs." *New York Times*. New York Times Company, 4 Jan. 2012. Web. 5 Jan. 2018.

7. Teresa Kroeger, et al. "The Class of 2016." *Economic Policy Institute*. Economic Policy Institute, 21 Apr. 2016. Web. 5 Jan. 2018.

8. Joseph Stiglitz. *The Great Divide*. New York: Norton, 2015. Print. 165.

9. Joseph Ferrie, et al. "Do Grandparents and Great-Grandparents Matter? Multigenerational Mobility in the US, 1910–2013." *National Bureau of Economic Research*. National Bureau of Economic Research, Sept. 2016. Web. 5 Jan. 2018.

CHAPTER 7. CLOSING THE GAP

1. "A Better Way: Our Vision for a Confident America." *A Better Way*. Speaker.gov, 7 June 2016. Web. 5 Jan. 2018.

2. Greg Kaufmann. "Why Achieving the American Dream Depends on Your Zip Code." *Talk Poverty*. Center for American Progress, 17 Dec. 2015. Web. 5 Jan. 2018.

3. Miles Corak. "Inequality from Generation to Generation: The United States in Comparison." *IZA Discussion Papers* 9929 (2012): 79–102. Print.

CHAPTER 8. RECENT TRENDS, FUTURE CHALLENGES

1. "About." *Occupy Wall Street*. Occupy Wall Street, n.d. Web. 5 Jan. 2018.

2. Anya Kamenetz. "Here's the Fine Print on the Country's Biggest-Ever Free College Plan." *NPR*. NPR, 11 Apr. 2017. Web. 5 Jan. 2018.

3. "Bernie's Announcement." *Bernie*. Friends of Bernie Sanders, 26 May 2015. Web. 5 Jan. 2018.

4. Daily News Staff. "Transcript of Donald Trump's 2016 Presidential Announcement." *Daily News*. NYDailyNews.com, 27 Apr. 2017. Web. 5 Jan. 2018.

5. Steven Greenhouse. "Driverless Future?" *American Prospect*. American Prospect, 21 Mar. 2017. Web. 5 Jan. 2018.

INDEX

ABOUT THE
AUTHORS

DUCHESS HARRIS, JD, PHD

Professor Harris is the chair of the American Studies department at Macalester College and curator of the Duchess Harris Collection of ABDO books. She is the author and coauthor of recently released ABDO books including *Hidden Human Computers: The Black Women of NASA*, *Black Lives Matter*, and *Race and Policing*.

Before working with ABDO, she authored several other books on the topics of race, culture, and American history. She served as an associate editor for *Litigation News*, the American Bar Association Section of Litigation's quarterly flagship publication, and was the first editor in chief of *Law Raza*, an interactive online journal covering race and the law, published at William Mitchell College of Law. She has earned a PhD in American Studies from the University of Minnesota and a JD from William Mitchell College of Law.

ELISABETH HERSCHBACH

Elisabeth Herschbach is an editor, writer, and translator from Washington, DC.